SHE IS THAT

Published by
Good Juju Publishing
Printed USA

ISBN: 9781673298345

there is no beginning and
there is no end

This little book was created for you
(I only know that because you are
reading it right now). I see *SHE IS THAT* as a
friend or a companion who is there when we feel
alone, need a change in perspective or a seed of
inspiration.

My poems come from a question/answer part of
myself. When I find myself wrestling with an idea
or a feeling I often pick up a pen to express. Both
my writings and drawings are from an unedited
part of myself, so in many ways I don't feel like
they are really from "me". They are from an un-
ending flow that sources from the unimaginable
mystery...
it is within me yet way beyond me
at the same time.

My wish for you is that this litle book comes to sit
with you when you need it. Maybe a drawing
illicits something or a poem or both. I hope you
feel me in them and know that you are not alone.

Love a Fellow Traveler,
Julia

Oh you, who walk under tender skies full of
lighted moons that ebb and flow,

Oh you, who walk on abundant ground that
grows your food
magically...

Oh you, who's waters roar past us
everyday we drink from her rivers and cry
near her streams...

Oh you, who lives with flying
songbirds and is a roommate of the fawns,

Oh you, who is me ...who is warmed by a
huge star in the sky millions of miles away

Oh me, who is gifted these crisp
morning moments to open or to close,
to give or to take ..

Oh me, who is you, we are given
another day , a whole other one!
where all possibilities await us

Oh me, oh you, oh us...
what is my, your, our next step...
in this moment,
just this little powerful
moment
right now?

POW!!
MAGIC
NOW

She is that.

We are exquisite, complicated yet
simple with many paradoxes within us.
I feel like I and we often reject this in
ourselves. What if our superpowers and our
weaknesses were integrated and our
wholeness was based on rejecting nothing?

What if we welcomed the parts
that are learning and growing
and that are still rageful, frightened,
crawling?

What would it be like if we decided that we
were really enough right this second?
not in a week or a month but NOW...

Shining
Luminous
Broken
Free
Open & Vital.

Like a roaring fire and a beautiful
ballet all at once.

I wish this for us.

Oh divine and mystical feminine...

Continue to awaken us from All
of our deep slumbers.

Show us what is real.

We have all come from the mother yet we
reject our very selves.

Help us
to realize that we are sacred.

We are all a part of her.
A never ending circle.

What we do to her
we surely do to
ourselves.

Fall

comes to earth and to us....
we let go of the retired parts of
ourselves
that no longer serve us
they no longer carry life
(we all know the places).

let them fall... dig deep and trust
the soil of your heart will have good compost
now
and soon very soon....

             you will find yourself a new.

Busted.

When She realized
She had put herself in a box
of her very own making
(self-imposed limitations).

She immediately then realized:
She was the one to get herself out.

So she did ...
it was as simple as that.

thank goodness.
.

be still my beating heart.

the
tree
and
her
were
old
friends...

...i love her...

She came to realize
She already was in the perfect place...

21

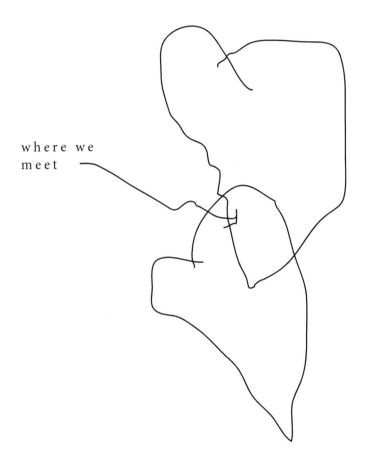

where we
meet

SHE HEARS ME. SHE LAUGHS HARDER WHEN I STOP. SHE MAKES ME THINK ABOUT THINGS ID RATHER NOT. THEN SOMEHOW I FEEL BETTER THAN BEFORE. I COUNT ON HER TO TELL THE TRUTH. TO RISE. TO FIND THE BRIGHT SIDE WHEN I ONLY SEE THE DARK SIDE. TO CRY WITH ME AND SIGH WITH ME. SHES BEAUTIFUL SMART AND SHE IS MY DEAREST FRIEND...FOREVER AND

there is NO END AND NO BEGINNING

She said,
as she walked through
the deep forest where there were
seemingly scary snakes and ferocious
chipmunks.

"No matter what...love and goodness
are the dominant forces. We have to dig
deep...not to close our hearts with the
pain we witness and feel.
The heart is forever stronger with an
aperture that is wide open.
Eyes wide open.
Fear is a trick."

All the chipmunks nodded in agreement
and the birds chirped
and the snakes were not
what she had once thought.

I never forgot her.

thank you

moon and stars

I love you.

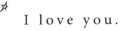

seek what makes you come alive.

(it is a sure sign)

my northstar is not like anyone elses...

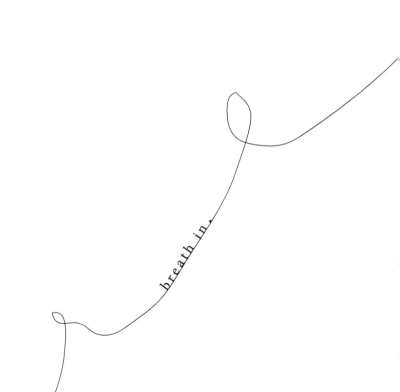

breath in.

breath out

What if winter was a woman...
and snow was her blanket

if the trees clothed in white dust
was her hair

if slipping on the ice was her dance
with you and her danger

snow forts her nest
the cold her need
spring her thermal core.

What then if she was and is a woman...
a force,
a reviver,
a silencer
a playground,
an unknown and
          a lover....

What then if winter was a woman...
how would you address her,
undress her or dress her?

Women or Winter
are not meant to be tamed.

No one is.
(No matter what they say)

ATTENTION.
TAKE NOTE OF
WHAT IT FEELS
LIKE TO BE ALIVE,
RIGHT NOW

a sign in
Ojai, CA.

She said,

"OH!   don't you see?
you'll never know
what will set you free....

and it is true my dear,
the darkest shadows are next to
the greatest light.

find the courage to remain."

the day and night of us.

runneth over

Weeping is part of it.
She knew grief.

Tenderness is born from a
softened fertile heart.
The earth weeps,
he weeps
babies cry.

She let her tears fall
willingly,

so the oceans could fill again.

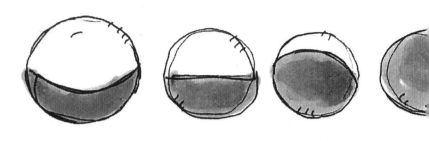

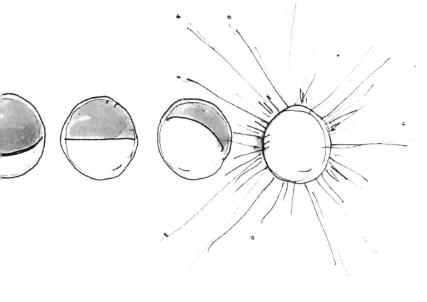

Moon beams.

Where the moon rises
the eagle swoops
and the raven calls.

It is there she ascends
from the inside out.

She reigns with the trees,
the stars and her heart.

...always with her heart.

She is the magic and mystery
of the night.

She is the shaman. The mistress, the
freedom fighter, the wild heart,
the birthing mother, the raging storm.

In the night
or the dark spaces of ourselves
we sometimes have fear yet,
the dark is the place of solace...

It is here where we navigate the quiet
stillness of our soul
(remember the quiet is not empty).
It is here where the imagination is born.

Our darkness is meant to be integrated and
welcomed like a dear friend,
not something to be avoided.

Find ways to accompany yourself through
the unlit spaces of your heart,
there are untold riches in there.

Just as the seed grows in the deep
incumbency of the earth,
as she awaits the waters to break her shell...
she soon rises,
to break ground
and enter the light.

You will to.
Trust.

Midnight Fruits.

Eclipse Girl.

Deep within the forest she found
orchards that no one knew about
the fruits were endless...

there was no she or he.

The sky was so blue.

She spins through space and stars.
She births continuously without effort.
She is silent.
She feeds & waters us and then
buries us back in her tender earth,
her breast.

...She is Mary.

Sometimes it is not easy.

You are smack dab in the dark and it is sketchy!
You are really wondering what the hell is
happening...
in those moments which come...

REMEMBER

There are unforeseen forces rearranging things
in such a way that your soul
will find a way to take flight once again,
with new fresh winds under her wings.

She will soar to new heights and she will carry
new pieces of light that she gathered while in
the dark.

Trust her
She will find a way...

She is fierce, just like you.

When lost in the world,
return to the song that is always singing in
your heart.

Listen deeper still.

And from the deepest place
in her soul's longing....

she wept
for this truth;

that the bounty of our spirits
are not bound by the body,
as so it appears

and then she wept again...
and from there

the most beautiful garden
GREW.

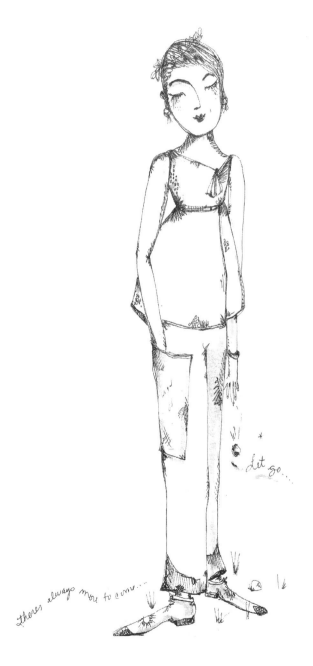

Let go...

there's always more to come...

i love you.

"Understand" she said

"there is nothing we do without
another

embrace what is before you..
lend a hand.

There are no coincidences.
You were born with much in mind.

NOW reach out past your comfort zone
it is most certainly not what you were born for.

You are born for navigating the
growth zone which demands your
open mind and heart.
Now go."

from that day on .....I grew.

I loved her.

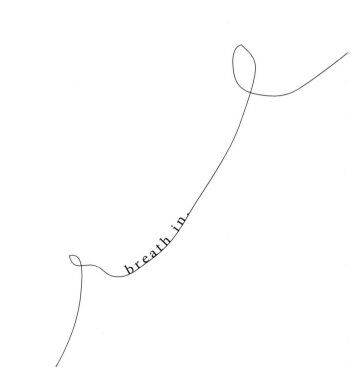

breath in

breath out.

spring!

oh you,

fresh, free bursting in me .....
you wash me,
grow me
and refine in me

.....new life.

(thank you so much...i will miss you when
i am gone.)

ok now,
it is s t o r y t i m e

part 1:

there was this girl
she carried
burdens
because that is the way she
thought it was...

she was very
uncomfortable.

(it was hard to watch)

69

part 2:

until the day it
began to dawn on her
that the story she had been
telling herself was simply
not true.

So...
she set down the burdens,
as well as her
        very own self.

she then began
listening...

    to her heart.

(the rocks seemed happier)

part 3:

and then step by step
her heart became
her trusty guide
her mind
a faithful servant
to her hearts desire

and from that day forward her
yoke was easy..

fruits flowed from her
                    effortlessly
and

a certain joy was
present in her...
        (no matter what.)

the end...

or.... perhaps a new beginning.

deep in her heart of hearts
there was a true gentleness

disguised
as toughness

but (really obviously)

bursting with a certain
loveliness.

YES
        that's her.

She danced
through
her life....

It was as if..
the more she was
true to herself
in the big and little ways
the more flowers grew from her,
the waters flowed
and
a crystal clear beauty became her.

*Remember to Read the signs...

You are an excellent person.

what you concentrate on, you get.

there are no exceptions.

Dear my deer,

please remember this ....

Her fruits are from the hidden depths
where darkness is not scary,
it is fertile.

When women rise, the fruits they bear
 have a heaviness and a longevity
related to them...

When we eat those fruits we are
replenished.
She is both fierce and soft.

with love,
The Divine Feminine

        (who has remained, yet is hidden
        from those who do not want to see her)

we

are

in

this

together.

do not believe the rhetoric.

just follow your soul....

she knows the way

(she really does).

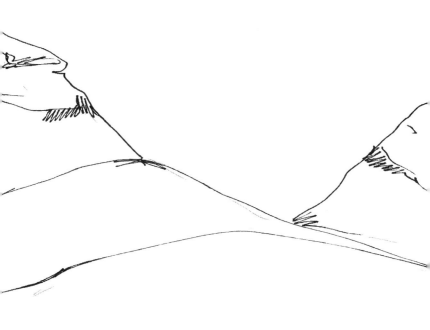

climb mountains.

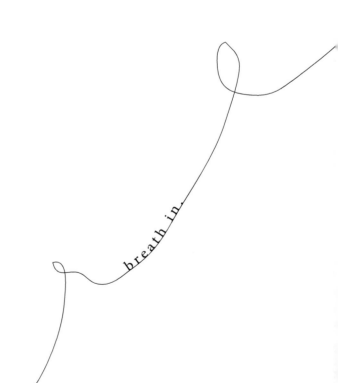

breath in.

breath out.

summer comes

and now
the heat of day
is born

growth blooms
there is ease and grace
integration
of fury and sorrow.

sunflowers dash
moonlight glows
the sun beams

and she dances
and dances

to the new day
ever fresh
on her breath

she radiates.

she is home.

And she knew that the greatest
contribution she could give was to first
ground her very own being everyday;
and then she could be the
true earth for others

holding steady...

even if there is turbulence.

go with the flow

run towards the fire, not away.

and we quiver at her anger.
where do you think it rises from?

MEET HER

it is ancient,
listen closely

it is the only remedy
for our ailment.

and for this.. she was born:
as a fire
to heat and melt
the layers of ice
(the cemented hurt and pain
lodged (in the heart of man)

YES,
she comes burning in flames,
no longer carrying shame

her flames
create a giant flood

as the flood ensues
the ocean is made
whole again

and the divisions clung to
(she, he, it, you, me)
that were killing her,
are now nonexistent.

WE
        ARE ONE.

her kind of magic
was my kind of magic.

GRACE

and with grace and intensity she moved
throughout her life

full of authentic joy and freedom
from the usual trappings.
she was gloriously dangerous

untamable

living like a dancer....
    rhythmic and fluid.

She came to realize...
that no matter her perceived conditions
(momentary for sure),
her natural state of grace was hers
and only hers to cultivate...

She naturally was brimming with
a vast courageous creativity.
like making honey day and night...
(the bees knew her well).

As she took time to receive
her natural bounty...

A natural ease and freedom
precededher and followed her
in and out of her many existences...

Suit or no suit...
naked or clothed,

it did not matter,
as grace suited her most of all.

So,
from that day forward
she owned it and flew far and wide...

open hearted and free

despite her naysayers,
        she never looked back.

thank goodness.

She had finally
come to a deep abiding place
within herself:

SHE TRUSTED LIFE

she came to see that
life was there for her:
cheering her on, picking
her up. addressing her sorrow
or walking beside her

her majestic self was now
brimming with an aliveness
and her momentum was
towards creation

she no longer took the "safe" road as
that was the least safe of all.

the weird thing is as she did that,
a great wind began to blow
through the fields reorchestrating
the leaves and the trees,
the sands and the vast lands

there was a belonging she now felt with
everything that surpassed any of the
separation and loneliness
she once believed to be true

she had became electric to
this very moment...
listening to the persistent magic
that was present and constantly
bursting with possibility.

Set your sights high!

She was unstoppable.

◈ JULIA JUNKIN ➤

Julia Junkin is an artist, poet and designer who has been creating art for over 20 years. Her work has been seen through out the country and in Nordstrom, Henri Bendel and Crate & Barrel. She is a gifted Sufi healer who bridges the gap between the spiritual and emotional realms. Julia offers the transformative power of creative expression as a path for awareness for herself and others.

www. juliajunkin.org

Made in United States
Orlando, FL
22 February 2023

30297500R00074